Oh Hello!

First published 2019
Copyright © Dave Ainsworth.

ISBN 978-0-244-78938-1

All rights reserved. The rights of Dave Ainsworth to be identified as the author of this work have been asserted in accordance with the Copyright Act 1991. No part of this publication may be reproduced, stored in a retrieval system or transmitted in any form or by any means, electronic, mechanical, photocopying, recording or otherwise, without prior permission in writing from the publisher. Public performance of this material is also prohibited without contractual agreement with the author or his representatives.

*This play is dedicated
to my sons Will and Tom*

Oh Hello!

Oh Hello! was originally staged at the Torch Theatre, Milford Haven in 2001 as part of the theatre's script development scheme with Dave Ainsworth in the role of Charles Hawtrey. The following year, it was part of the Edinburgh Fringe Festival (Venue 13) where it received a number of very positive reviews. A tour of Wales followed. Another successful tour was staged in 2004.

The play was revived in 2015 by the Torch Theatre's artistic director Peter Doran who had directed the original and subsequent productions. Jamie Rees took the title role and *Oh Hello!* was a sell out for its three-week run at the Assembly Rooms, Edinburgh Fringe. This feat was repeated the following year.

> "... While Dave Ainsworth offers a fair share of behind-the-scenes anecdotes, his solo play is actually a moving study in decline and self-delusion." *The Stage*

Oh Hello!

"Dave Ainsworth's Fringe hit tribute to Charles Hawtrey….." *The Daily Mail*

"This bio-play is funny and sad in equal measure. Dave Ainsworth charts Charles Hawtrey's decline sensitively, never allowing the poignancy to overwhelm the humour, making Oh Hello! an extremely enjoyable show – and definitely one to make time to see this Fringe." *Three Weeks*

"Dave Ainsworth has managed to write a play which covers a great deal of ground in around an hour, and does so with great skill and economy." *Chris Abbott, Sardines*

Charles Hawtrey

Charles Hawtrey is best remembered for having starred in the phenomenally successful Carry On series of films that spanned the 1950's to the late 1970's. The films made an enormous amount of money for the failing British film industry and made the producer Peter Rogers a millionaire. Charles Hawtrey had starred in 23 of them, but, like the rest of the cast received a paltry salary.

Hawtrey had learnt his craft from working with the legendary Will Hay. He starred in four films with him – *Good Morning Boys!* (1937), *Where's the Fire?* (1940), *The Ghost of St Michael's* (1941) and *The Goose Steps Out* (1942). After a lull, Hawtrey was cast in the popular television series *The Army Game* that ran from 1957 until 1961 and he was cast in the very first Carry On film, *Carry on Sergeant* in 1958. He, along with his fellow co-stars, were the lynchpin of the success of the Carry On series. Hawtrey was often cast in unlikely roles and his appearances were always cleverly timed to maximise the comedic impact, using his catchphrase, "'Oh Hello!" to full effect.

After he was dropped in 1972 following an altercation over billing, his career faded away and his addiction to alcohol took a grip. He died in a nursing home after suffering a fall in 1988.

By all accounts, Charles Hawtrey was certainly difficult to work with, yet in spite of this, most of the Carry On cast retained a genuine fondness for him. Joan Sims and Hattie Jacques were always kind to him – as was Barbara Windsor, who described Hawtrey as being 'the best comic of the team.'

Oh Hello!

Dave Ainsworth

The original 2001 production at the Torch Theatre, Milford Haven and subsequent tours and Edinburgh Fringe residency at Venue 13:

Charles Hawtrey – Dave Ainsworth
Writer – Dave Ainsworth
Director – Peter Doran

The 2015 revival, including Edinburgh Fringe residency at Assembly Rooms in that year and 2016:

Charles Hawtrey – Jamie Rees
Writer – Dave Ainsworth
Director – Peter Doran

PROLOGUE

Charles Hawtrey stumbles onto the set with a walking stick. We see a table with a photograph on it. A chair next to it. A comfortable armchair with a drinks trolley beside it complete the set.

He picks up the photograph. He puts down the photograph, picks up a bottle of lemonade and then speaks to the photograph:

HAWTREY: This is my friend (*Takes a swig*). But rather like some friends this is not all that it seems. It may look unmistakably like a lemonade bottle but well, let's just say what is within is certainly not lemonade. Outside – innocence, inside – delightful wickedness. *(Takes a swig)* Not much of a friend you might say, but you'd be wrong. It's the only one I have. The only one I have left… There's so much cardboard in this business, so much deceit… This is the only friend I want.

(Pause) Sometimes, just sometimes, I can hear my mother's voice…

FADE TO BLACK

SCENE 1

Charles Hawtrey's home in London, 1962. He enters brightly.

HAWTREY: Oh Hello! I bumped into a journalist this morning. He said, "It's Charles Hawtrey!" I said "Yes". He said, "Mister Hawtrey, can I ask you one or two questions?" I said "Of course." He then asked me if I had enjoyed my career as a film comedian. I said, "Yes, but my life is far from over. I have," I said "a lot more to offer." I've just finished this new Carry On — *Carry on Regardless*. Oh, it's a credible little film I suppose but it's really rather a minor affair I'm afraid. I had a few interviews today so I suppose I deserve a drop.

(Pours a glass) Cheers! I said to them, "Actually, I prefer the medium of film. Ideally I'd like to work exclusively in films." I said that one could be easily over-exposed in

Oh Hello!

television. They then asked me about the film and I said, "Oh, it's the funniest Carry On so far." I said, "The humour is more mature, more sustained and more plentiful than ever!" All rubbish of course, but I think they swallowed it (*Has a drink*).

In truth it's all very mundane and the writing's not terribly good either. I said to the writer, I said, "Don't be afraid to give me a few funny lines now and again. I am a comedian, you know — I can cope!" Then there's been this problem over the billing!

I said to the producer Peter Rogers, I said, "I've been in your series of films since the first one." I said, "Not only that but I have a far wider experience in film than any other member of the cast." I said, "I've worked with Will Hay, I've worked with Groucho Marx, I've been directed by Alfred Hitchcock. I've been a star since the Thirties, surely I deserve top billing!"

He said, "Charles, with the best will in the

world, I can't bill you above Sid James!" I said, "Why not? Sid James has never been directed by Alfred Hitchcock!", "Ah, but he's been in more films than you!". I said, "Peter, with respect, it's not the quantity here, it's the quality love. I have been in *quality* films since the 1920's whereas Sid…"

The best years of my life, those films with Will Hay. He was the best comedian — the master. When I was working with him, I was at the top of my profession in the real film industry. Not this bastardized version we see now. I was in some of the greatest films of that time – *The Ghost of St. Michael's, The Goose Steps Out, Passport to Pimlico* – Now those were *real* comedy films.

I said to Rogers, I said, "And what about The Army Game?" I said, "If that's not success, I'd like to know what is! If that's not fame, what is?" That television programme was the epitome of success. But Rogers wouldn't listen. No, I think he thought that I was trying to undermine Sid James, but I wasn't.

No, it did no good. I could tell Rogers wasn't going to budge so I left it to my agent to sort out. In the end, it was futile; they refused – refused – to give me top billing. So that was that! I said, and I was quite witty here, I said, "well, you can carry on without me!"

FADE TO BLACK

SCENE II

The same. 1964. Weeks later.

HAWTREY: I met a nice boy on set this morning – name's Nigel. Very nice, very considerate. *He* said he's a runner. I said, "Well don't you worry, I won't be running away from you!" I'm sure he blushed, but I didn't care! I noticed that the director Gerald Thomas was peering over his newspaper and I'm sure he heard. But I don't care. Why should I care what he thinks! Some of them just pretend to care, but they don't really. They just pretend. However, there are some who are genuine, especially some of the young ones.

(*Excitable*) Jim Dale came up to me during lunch and said, "I'm learning a lot from you. I'm learning a lot about comic business."

(*Flattered and modest, but not really*) I said,

"Well, it's all tricks. Mind you," I said "it's an awful lot of tricks. It's the stare, the look: it's the reaction and the pause. It can be visual or verbal but it must have timing and, above all, it must have style." Jim was listening intently. I said, "Mind you, I've had the best teachers. Will Hay for instance, taught me an enormous amount. Just by watching him, listening to him, I couldn't fail to learn the basics. I was in four films with him and with him I learnt the essentials of film comedy." "And now," said Jim "I can learn from you!"

Now there, I thought was a boy who will go somewhere. I said to him, I said, "You don't want to be stuck doing this shit for long, you want to be out there doing something of substance." I thought I should know! I was at the Old Vic... ... for a bit.

(*He sits*) It seems a bit strange being back on set. Yes, I'm back with Peter Rogers and his Carry On debacle. We're making this new one. It's quite a clever little parody on all those James Bond films. I'm playing special agent

Charlie Bind. Double o —Oh! (*Slight pause*)

Why, I'm back I'm not sure because the atmosphere is... rather strained against me. There's some sort of campaign, some sort of whispering campaign building up. There seems to be, and I'm not imagining this, a general opinion that I am drinking too much on set. (*He drinks from his glass*) Me! Of course, I know where all this is coming from. I know alright.

(*He stands*) On the last one, the last Carry On, Kenny Williams comes marching up to me and says, "Oh, you're pissed! You're completely and utterly pissed!" Of course, I tried to laugh it off, but she kept screaming, "Oh, it's disgusting!".

I thought, "Ooh! Get her! Talk about – Hello kettle, pot calling!". I think she was just doing it to impress the others. I admitted I may have had one or two, but Kenny wasn't listening, he just went on and on. "It's so unprofessional! I will not work with amateurs!" Amateurs! Well, that was that I flounced out. I won't be insulted like that especially by Kenny who I regard as a friend, a confidant. I mean, it's not as if he's perfect! True, I may like a drink or two and I've been known to seek out the company of men, but at least I'm honest about it! We all know that Kenny has to run away to Morocco every time he gets an erection!

(Going over to the drinks trolley, pours another drink) They all drink – all of them. Even the girls, even Joanie. They all drink!

Besides, I had to have a drink that particular day because we were filming the boat sequence. A tiny little rowing boat floating in the tank. I thought, "Well, I'm not doing this without a drink or two!" Very uncomfortable it was nonetheless. There was me, Kenny, Bernie Cribbins, the Mills gal and a cow... all cramped into this tiny rowing boat. Kenny Williams kept up the sarcasm all day. He kept asking Gerry if he could sit next to the cow rather than me. He said the cow had fresher breath! Not that I care. Kenny only really makes remarks like that to make himself more interesting.

(He sits down and has another drink) Oh but it was a horrible day! It's disgraceful the way they treat us all in these films. (*Walking back over to the armchair*) And they don't care about any pain or discomfort you may be suffering. Today was a case in point although they wouldn't see it that way.

(Slight pause. He stands) There they were carrying us down this conveyor belt and being pushed here and there and generally being molested in the most obscene way. And, apparently, halfway through the shot, I passed out — completely fainted. They had to stop filming, whilst they pulled me down onto the set floor. Pure exhaustion, it was obviously pure exhaustion. I was just pulling myself back into the land of the living when the new girl, Barbara Windsor shouts out, "Get him a brandy! For Gawds sake get him a brandy!" And Gerald said, "It

was probably the brandy that did this in the first place!" and everyone started laughing. (*He walks back to the armchair and sulks*)

I don't think it was the brandy. I mean, I had had one or two. Well, I had to in order to carry out the things they were asking me to do. Hypocrites – the lot of them!

Still, I won my little battle with Peter Rogers. He practically begged me back into the fold. He had to in the end. All the critics said they missed me in *Carry on Cruising*. One of them said it may be the first one in colour but in being the first one without Charles Hawtrey some of that colour was lost. I rather liked that. So, anyway, I'm back and the agreement is I will be guaranteed third billing for this and all subsequent pictures. Third billing... after Sid and Kenny. The pay's slightly up too – £4,000 per picture. (*Slight pause, then walks back to the drinks trolley*) It's still pitiful of course, but any increase must be deemed a major victory when dealing with this lot.

I brought mother in with me today and she went on and on about getting me ready for school and such-like. I don't think Barbara knew what to do. In the end, when it came to my scene, I locked mother in the dressing room with a cup of tea. Well, it's best. I usually do that because if I'm not there to watch her, she does tend to wander off…
..She's having a lie down now bless her.

Pause. He looks at the carrier bag by his feet and picks it up.

Oh, look at this! I had completely forgotten about this! I asked the girl in the canteen for a few bits and pieces for the cat. Left overs, you know.

He takes out a sandwich for the cat, splits it open and takes out a piece of sardine. He looks at it and neatly pops it in his mouth.

Hmm! Not bad.

SCENE III

The same. 1966.

HAWTREY: (*Looking up*) Is that my mother calling? (*It isn't*) No.

She's been calling out a lot this morning. She hasn't been herself for days. I thought that bringing her to the studio would cheer her up. It usually does.

When I took her to the studio last week I put her in the dressing room as usual but, because I was a little late for my shot, I forgot to lock the door behind me. Of course, she left her tea and walked out looking for me. She was wandering round the corridors saying, "Has anyone seen my Charlie? I've got his tea ready and everything!" She certainly covered a lot of ground because one of the continuity girls found her outside the canteen. The girl pointed mother in the right direction, but she veered off onto the set next door. Eventually Barbara found her. There was mummy asking John Gielgud if he had seen "her little Charlie?" I can't imagine what Johnny thought. Apparently, he was very good about the whole thing.

He crosses to the table and picks up a film script and starts thumbing through it.

The role they've given me this time is little more than a cameo. Oh, I've done what I can with it, but you can't make a silk purse out of a sow's ear, can you? I mean, I only appear for five minutes! Seemingly I wouldn't have got that if it weren't for the powers that be. They tell me that my role – Dan Dann the lavatory man – was offered initially to someone else and that I would not be in the film at all. Well, a newspaper got wind of this and they let it be known that a Carry On film without my presence would be a travesty. This, in turn, promoted the film distributor to put pressure on Rogers to make sure that I was included. Can you imagine! Nat Cohen ticking off Peter Rogers! Naturally, Rogers laughed it off and pretended that it was never his intention not to cast me. Hypocrite! Rogers said, "Just having Charles Hawtrey's face in the film is worth every penny!" Penny's right – because that's all they're paying: pennies! And there's Peter Bloody Rogers driving to the studio in a Rolls Royce! It makes you sick! The man's drunk with power!

(Excited, pulling his chair to the centre) Oh… now… talking about Rolls Royces, an extraordinary thing happened last week! There I was walking to the Studio, minding my own business when this huge Rolls Royce stops by the side of me. I always walk the last bit. When I'm filming here I leave the house in Hounslow and the I take the train to Uxbridge and that's where I start my little trek. Anyway, there I was and this chauffer-driven Rolls Royce stops right in front of me. The window rolls down and I see that it's… Larry – it's Laurence Olivier who's on his way to film some historical piece on the

neighbouring set. "Charles!" he cried. "Don't they give you a car?" I said, "A car! You must be joking! They don't even give me the bus fare!" "It's outrageous!" he said and then he offered me a lift to Pinewood. I accepted at once and I sat down beside him.

He said, "What's in the bag?" I said, "Oh you know, the usual; woodbines, The Times, my script and a couple of bottles of lemonade...". He said, "Lemonade!" I said, "Yes, very good for the throat, lemonade." And he nodded. Well, I certainly wasn't going to tell him what was really in the bottles, was I? Larry then went on and on about how disgraceful it was that we were being paid so little when so much money was being made with these films. Well, he's right there. They tell me that *Carry on Nurse* was the biggest grossing film of 1959 and that every film since has made millions. They've all made millions. Larry said, "You get little money, no luxuries — it's a disgrace!"

Of course when I went to the studio I told

them all about. I said, "Larry told me that he would not stand for such treatment." "Oh," said Kenny "so that's why they don't cast him in the Carry On films!".

I shut up then I opened my copy of The Times. l read while Kenny went on and on about his on-going battle with hemorrhoids. *(Pause)* I wonder if the cat's got fleas?

LIGHTS FADE TO BLACK

SCENE IV

Hawtrey's new home in Deal. 1970.

HAWTREY: Do you like it? It's not *The Ritz*, I know, but it's certainly very adequate. I bought this little place in Deal because... Well, it's quiet and away from London and I'm thinking ahead you see – retirement. I thought, I'll use this as my little base, unless I go to Australia of course. I'm very big down under, so they tell me. Perhaps, I'll go there, chance my arm. (*Slight pause*) But this is nice. It's a shame my mother... (*He stops. The memory is painful.*) She's not here now... she's gone. But she's still here in spirit – speaking of which – (*He pours himself a glass*) Cheers! I have so few pleasures these days. (*He looks around puzzled.*) What was I doing?

He starts to clean up with a brush along the front of the stage. He stops.

D'you know, the budgets for these Carry On films may have got bigger but the wages certainly haven't. I'm still only on £4,000 a picture – It's a disgrace! The money's not moved in over eight years! Then again, Joanie tells me she's still on £2,500! I mean, it's not as if the money's not there. Rogers and Thomas are positively awash with cash! Someone told me they've spent over £200,000 on this *Carry On* fucking... (*Forgets the word*)... *Henry* and it'll go on to make millions like the rest of them. The only ones who will benefit will be the backers and Peter Rogers and Gerald Thomas of course. They'll be the only winners. We won't see a penny that's for sure. It's all greed, greed, bloody greed with that lot... (*He starts to clean again, but stops sharply*) And, do you know, Peter Rogers had the temerity to say that I should take a lower billing for the last Carry On, *Carry on Loving*. He said, "Charles, the role is so slight, it doesn't warrant third billing." I said, "That's immaterial. I have been promised third billing and as far as I'm concerned that promise should be kept." He said, "But Charles, Hattie's role is so much bigger..." I said – *(He's about to swear, but stops)* I said nothing. I wouldn't budge. He knew I wouldn't budge. Kenny thought that I was being childish. Silly old queen.

(He drops the dustpan and sits) Actually, I think Kenny was still mad at me for taking a shine to a boy he fancied on the set of Camping. He was a props boy by the name of Alf. Angelic creature. Charming, quite, quite charming. I bought him little presents, you know chocolate and such like and Kenny was furious. He said to me, "Must you make yourself so obvious, so transparent." Jealousy, pure jealousy. Later on, I heard him talking to the boy; he said, "You want to watch Charlie! He'll make a pass at you before long." And the props boy replied, "It wouldn't worry me!" Ah, delightful boy – charming!

(He has a quick drink) I had an exhausting day today. There was a party to celebrate the 21st Carry On film, this new one *Carry on*

Oh Hello!

Henry. In the film I play Sir Roger de Lodgerley who is suspected of having an affair with one of Henry VIII's queens. There's a nice piece of dialogue actually. Sid James who's playing the king is interrogating me. He says to me, "Well, Sir Roger? Have you been dallying with the Queen?" I say, "Certainly not, Sire!" And then, he says, "Your hand on it?" And then I say, "Not even a finger on it!" I'm sure it'll work.

Anyway going back to this party at the Dorchester, the first thing I noticed was that there weren't many there. Not many actors, but quite a few journalists mind. At one point one of the photographers said, "Mr. Hawtrey, could we have a photo of you putting your arm around Barbara Windsor?" I said, "I'd rather put my arm around a gentleman. Couldn't you find me one?" I really was naughty. Barbara didn't know where to look.

In the end, they took a photograph of me between Joan Sims who's playing Queen

Marie and Barbara Windsor who's playing Queen Bet. Kenny shouted behind us "Oh, look at those three queens!"

(Pause. He sits, quietly) I walked away and sat by myself. Later on, I asked one of the waitresses to pack up some of the leftovers in a carrier bag. Well, waste not, want not. I kept thinking, the budgets may be up, but my salary isn't — grab what you can, that's my motto! It's a disgrace! I've worked with Will Hay, I've been directed by Alfred Hitchcock.

(Pause) I fell asleep on set again. When I woke up there was no one there.

LIGHTS FADE TO BLACK

SCENE V

The same. 1972.

HAWTREY: I had visitors the other day. Nice, because I don't get many visitors these days. There I was still in my under vest and pajama bottoms when I heard a knock on my door. It was very inconvenient — not only was I not dressed but I had just put my lunch, a steak and kidney pie, out on the table. It was Kenneth Williams and his friends Tom and Clive. I said, "Oh, come in, come in!" but Kenny seeing that I wasn't really ready for company said they'd pop out for a couple of drinks until I was ready. I think he was in one of his brusque moods. Very nose in the air he was. As I closed the door behind them, I distinctly heard him say that my home smelt of cat's piss.

I got dressed and rushed down my lunch before they returned. It was only when I finished shaving that I remembered asking them to call down and see me. I'd completely forgotten about it. They had also offered to give me a lift to London. When they returned I opened a bottle of bubbly and gave them a good look over the place. I showed them everything. I even showed a few of my more intimate magazines. Well, I don't care...

It was then that Kenny said they would have to make a move and I said, "Oh, just give me a few moments to pack a little bag." Kenny said, "What?" I said, "I'll just pack an overnight bag." I really don't think he remembered I was going with them. Tom said to Kenny, "Oh, Charlie's coming back with us, we promised him a lift." Kenny sniffed, "Oh..." and looked very annoyed. "Well, *I* didn't know you were coming!" Little Miss Moody was terribly quiet the whole way up and seemed very perturbed every time I made Tom or Clive laugh. He was still sulking when we got to Victoria. Completely ruined the weekend!

Now then, on Monday something rather extraordinary happened. Peter Rogers phoned my agent and told him that my request to hold top billing for this television Christmas show had been turned down. What a cheek! With neither Kenneth nor Sid James available, I (as third in line so to speak), should therefore be top of the bill. But Rogers didn't see it that way. He said, "Charles, with the best will in the world, I can't bill you above Hattie Jacques!" I said, "Why not, I appear before her in the films and I've been in more of them. I've been in all of them bar one. I'm the established star," I said. I said, "Even alphabetically I win because Hawtrey comes before Jacques." I said, "It makes no sense." But he wasn't having any of it. I said to my agent, I said, "I've been in films since the 1920's and I've never been treated as shabbily as this. I've worked with Will!" I said, "I've been directed by Hitchcock!"

The upshot was that Rogers wouldn't budge, although he conceded he really wanted me in the show. I thought, "Right, if you want me so much you'll come round and give me top billing." So, I said to my agent, "If Rogers rings again, tell him I'm having tea in Bourne and Hollingsworth." They do a very nice tea there. Anyway, there I was just stabbing out a woodbine when one of the waitresses came over and said, "Mr. Hawtrey, there's a telephone call for you." It wasn't Rogers, it was the director Gerald Thomas. He said "Charles, this is it. You have to make up your mind finally right now, before you hang up. Will you accept second billing or won't you?" I said, "No." No, as simple as that. No. So, that was that no more Carry On for me.

And after I told my agent, I thought – "Good. I'm well shot of the whole bloody lot of them!" *(Pause. He picks up the photo)* I'm rather glad actually. *(Pause)* I'll be better off without them.

LIGHTS FADE TO BLACK

SCENE VI

The same. 1977.

HAWTREY: I had a dream last night that I was being sick on the set of a Carry On film. There I was in agony, being sick into a bucket. The absurd thing was that when I woke I realised it wasn't a dream at all – it was a recollection. The whole thing had happened. This wasn't a dream, it was a memory. And then I thought back to the many times I had been in this situation. The situation of being sick on the set. I think the worst time was one terrible afternoon. I had been drinking quite a bit. Too much probably and Barbara Windsor came over. All sweetness and light, all ready to help me out – clean up after me, hold my hand and such-like.... "Come on Charlie, let me help you." "Oh why don't you just piss off – you're always trying to be so kind and good to everyone!" She left me to it. I just wanted to die ... I ***just*** wanted to die... (*Pours himself a drink*) Oh, it's quite alright. I haven't had one all day. *(Drinks the glass in one gulp)*

Yesterday, I poured two glasses of sherry – one for me and one for my... then I suddenly remembered...

(Pause)

(Pours another glass) Not that I'm lonely, you understand. I don't want you to get that impression. I can go anywhere in this town – anywhere – and people will chat to me. "Oh, don't you miss doing the Carry Ons?" they all ask. I say, "No." And I must say I'm rather pleased to see how badly these films are now doing without me. I wouldn't go back for anything. No – retirement suits me...

Oh, I've done the odd piece here and there, but I'm basically a man of leisure these days. I'm still asked to do the occasional film part. I was offered the role of Sir Henry Baskerville in Peter Cook's new movie, but I turned it down. And you'll never guess who's been given the role in the end – Kenneth Bloody Williams.

Now oddly enough, Kenny came to see me the other day. I hadn't seen him in ages. He came with Tom and Clive. I took them to see the sights. I've been banned again from *The Saracen's Head*. They over-reacted terribly. They said I abused the barmaid after I chatted up every man in the pub. Outrageous! (*Slight pause*) Although I do recall calling someone a charlatan and throwing a glass …. somewhere…

Kenny, Tom, Clive and I went for a stroll along the front… "Yahoo! Hello boys!" I waved at everyone as usual… fishermen, sailors, everyone… Of course, I could see that Kenny was irritated as usual. He said, "Must you parade yourself so openly?" I said, "Well, I'm bringing a little bit of colour to their drab lives. They love me here Kenny, they simply adore me!" The sky was clear, the sun was warm… I haven't seen Kenny since then.

(*Slight pause*) Haven't seen anyone really. Well no one important. Not really. I mean you can't include the postman, can you? Not that I'm lonely, you understand. I'm not... Really, I'm not...

LIGHTS FADE TO BLACK

SCENE VII
Deal. Hawtrey is on the phone. Days later.

HAWTREY: Oh Hello! Deal Taxi Company?... Splendid... Yes, that's right! Charles Hawtrey! ...Now would you be an absolute treasure and deliver a few things to me? That's right, the usual address. Now then, I'd like six bottles of gin, four sherry —two sweet, two dry, two bottles of bubbly, no, let's make that three and a tray of tonics. Yes, that's right.... Sorry? Having a party? No, I'm not having a party.... Just in case, you know.... Half an hour? Splendid. *(Puts the phone down)* Charming boy, so efficient...

Long pause. He looks around the room and focuses on an unseen object. He is talking to his mother.

That's right, Mummy, he said half an hour, then you and I can have a little drinkie. Sherry, is it? No. No, not today... No filming today, no. No, that journalist has gone now. He's gone! He asked me all the usual questions. He seemed quite surprised by the amount of work I've done. I told him, I said —

He stops sharply. He realises what he is doing. He looks afraid.

You're not here, are you? No one's here, are they? *(He sits slowly and picks up the photo)* There's nobody here...

LIGHTS FADE SLOWLY

SCENE VII

Hawtrey at home. 1984.
The flat has been burnt out, guttered.
He looks old and tired.

HAWTREY: One of the nurses said, "You could have been killed in that fire, you could have been killed!" I said nothing. I was thinking, "My life may have been saved, but I've lost a great deal more besides." The fire did more than just destroy my home. In a way, it destroyed me as well. The way I'm perceived I mean, the way I appear. There I was in a national newspaper, a picture of me taken minutes after the incident with a blanket draped over my shoulders. I looked... Dreadful. Old and unwanted. And I don't want to be old and unwanted. I want to be cherished, I want to be loved...

All of it twisted against me: a collection of half-truths that questioned my morals and my sanity. All of it reveling in my discomfort.

Yesterday I sat in the pub until three. The landlady made it clear she didn't want me there. She said, "I'll only serve you if you promise to behave yourself. I don't want no more incidents! I don't want the police in here again, thank you very much! And I want my money up front, I don't want you cadging drinks off me or my customers either!"

When the fire happened I... Well, I don't recall all the events, but I do remember being carried out by a fireman while my home, my lovely home burnt down around me.

(Getting up) I said, "Let me back in there!" A fireman said, "What's the matter Charlie? Forgotten your woodbines?" I said, "NO! There's a boy in my bed!" *(Pause)* I wanted, I really wanted, to say something amusing to the firemen... "Come on, show us your hose!"... (*Defeated*) But I couldn't. *(Pause)* As I stood there with the blanket flung across

my bare shoulders, I was suddenly aware of the prying eyes, the stares, the whispers. People were seeing me as a senile old man, an oddity, a pervert…

(He sits) And as I sat there in the pub, I heard the landlady say, "Oh, don't buy him a drink, you'll never get one in return! He's a tight-wad he is!" I thought, "How did I end up like this?" That's why I went back home, you see… I went back to mummy. I thought, "At least she'll understand." She's the only one left see…

LIGHTS FADE TO BLACK

SCENE IX

A nursing home outside Deal. 1988.
Stage is bare.

HAWTREY: (*Off*) Nurse! Nurse!

(He enters slowly with a stick) The doctor said I have blood clots in my veins. He said, "Amputation's the only option." I said, "No thank you." I said, "I've been legless more often than you've had hot dinners.... " Which was quite witty, actually. He said, "You'll die if we don't amputate!" I said, "I think I'd rather die with my boots on, thank you."

(Moves to centre, then) He said, "You were in all those Carry On films, weren't you?" I said, "Oh, but I've done more than that!" I said, "I've worked with Will Hay, I've been directed by Alfred Hitchcock." *(He starts to move. Slight pause.)* And then he said, "Who's Will Hay...?"

Oh Hello!

HE EXITS AS LIGHTS GO TO BLACK

THE END.

Printed in Great Britain
by Amazon